ANIMALS

Dolphins

by Kevin Holmes

Content Consultant:
Dana Carnegie
Dolphin Research Center

Bridgestone Books

an imprint of Capstone Press

Bridgestone Books are published by Capstone Press
818 North Willow Street, Mankato, Minnesota 56001
http://www.capstone-press.com

Library of Congress Cataloging-in-Publication Data
Holmes, Kevin J.
    Dolphins/by Kevin J. Holmes.
    p. cm.--(Animals)
    Includes bibliographical references (p. 23) and index.
    Summary: An introduction to dolphins, covering their physical characteristics,
habits, prey, and relationship to humans.
    ISBN 1-56065-574-7
    1. Dolphins--Juvenile literature. [1. Dolphins.] I. Title.
II. Series: Animals (Mankato, Minn.)
QL737.C432H64   1998
599.53--dc21

          97-12205
          CIP
          AC

Photo credits
Innerspace Visions/Doug Perrine, cover, 4, 6, 8, 10, 14, 18
International Stock/Chad Ehlers, 20
Cheryl R. Richter, 16
Visuals Unlimited/Ken Lucas, 12

Table of Contents

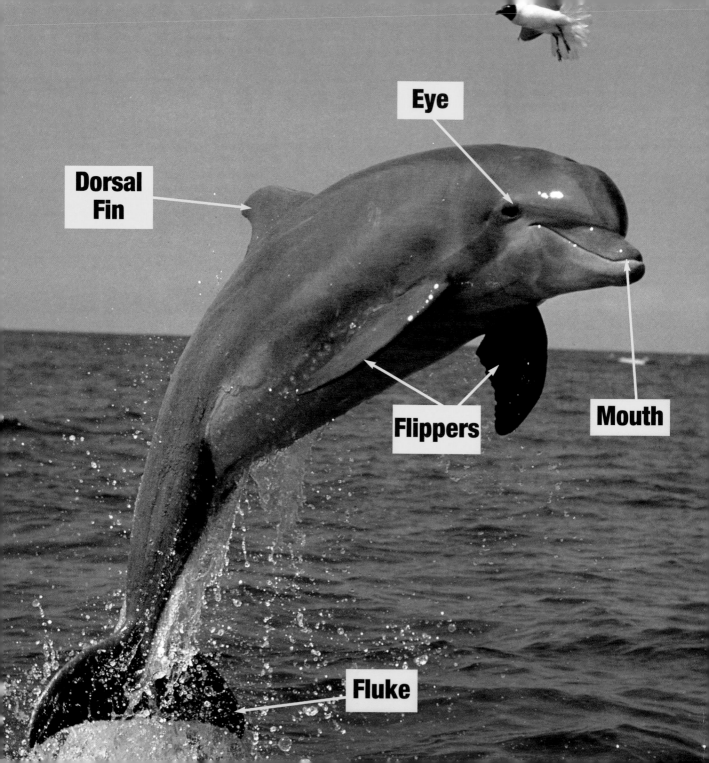

Eye

Dorsal Fin

Mouth

Flippers

Fluke

Fast Facts

Kinds: There are more than 30 kinds of dolphins. Some dolphins live in freshwater. Others live in saltwater.

Range: Freshwater dolphins live in the rivers of Asia and South America. Saltwater dolphins live in all the oceans of the world.

Habitat: Dolphins live in freshwater or saltwater.

Food: Most dolphins eat mainly fish. Some dolphins eat squid and crabs.

Mating: Female dolphins give birth every two to three years. Females usually give birth to one young dolphin at a time.

Young: Young dolphins are called calves. Calves can see, hear, and swim on their own at birth.

Dolphins

Dolphins look like fish, but they are really mammals. A mammal is a warm-blooded animal with a backbone. Warm-blooded means that the animal's body heat stays the same. Its body heat does not change with the outside weather.

Because they are mammals, dolphins breathe air. Their young are born alive. Young dolphins drink their mothers' milk.

There are more than 30 kinds of dolphins. Some live in freshwater. Others live in saltwater. Freshwater dolphins live in the rivers of Asia and South America. Saltwater dolphins live in all the oceans of the world.

Dolphins act in different ways. Most dolphins are very active. They jump high into the air. They bow ride at the front of boats. A bow ride is when a dolphin rides the boat's waves. The waves help push the dolphins through the water.

Some dolphins like to jump high into the air.

Appearance

Dolphins can be several different colors. Some are gray, black, or white. Others are even pink. All dolphins have streamlined bodies. Streamlined means shaped to move more quickly through the water. Their body shape helps them swim fast.

Most dolphins have fins on their backs. These are called dorsal fins. They also have one flipper on each of their sides. The flippers are like arms. They help dolphins steer through the water.

Dolphins have tails called flukes. Flukes are flat. Dolphins move their flukes up and down. This moves them through the water.

Dolphins' ears are small holes near their eyes. Dolphins must swim to the water's surface to breathe air. They breathe through blowholes. A blowhole is an opening on top of a dolphin's head. Dolphins open their blowholes to take in air. They close their blowholes when they dive underwater.

Dolphins have flippers that help them steer.

Echolocation

Dolphins use sound for many things. They click, whistle, and squeak. They use these sounds to talk to each other. Dolphins use different sounds to find prey. Prey are animals hunted and eaten for food. Most dolphins can see well. But sound also helps them find their way around.

Dolphins use sound during echolocation. Echolocation means the dolphins send out thousands of clicks. These clicks bounce off objects that are in front of the dolphins. The echoes help them know where objects are located. Dolphins learn many things from the echoes. Echoes tell them the objects' size, shape, speed, and direction. They can even tell what objects are made of.

Scientists believe that echolocation may mix up the dolphins' prey. Groups of dolphins hunt together. They send out thousands of clicks when they surround fish. Fish may become mixed up by the noise. Then dolphins catch them easily.

Groups of dolphins hunt together.

Eating and Enemies

Most dolphins prefer to eat fish. Some dolphins eat squid and crabs.

Dolphins have several ways of catching their food. One way is fish whacking. Fish whacking is when dolphins use their tails to hit fish. Sometimes this kills fish. Sometimes it only knocks fish out. Either way, dolphins eat the fish. Some dolphins follow fishing boats. People on fishing boats often throw unwanted fish overboard. The unwanted fish make an easy meal for dolphins.

Sharks and people are dolphins' main enemies. But dolphins sometimes fight back. A group of adult dolphins may ram a shark if it attacks. Dolphins' hard snouts damage the shark's body. A snout is the front part of an animal's head.

People hurt dolphins, too. Many dolphins get caught in fishing nets. The nets trap the dolphins underwater. The dolphins cannot breathe if they cannot surface. Then they may drown.

Most dolphins prefer to eat fish.

Young Dolphins

Female dolphins give birth every two to three years. Young dolphins are called calves. Females usually have only one calf at a time. Females help their calves to the surface for their first breaths.

Calves can see, hear, and swim on their own. But calves also depend on their mothers. Calves need their mothers' milk and protection. Young dolphins may nurse from their mothers for three years. They may live with their mothers for many years after that.

Many dolphins live in groups. These groups are called pods. Older females form pods with other females. Adult females help each other raise the calves. Older males form pods with other males. Dolphins stay together in pods for safety.

Healthy dolphins guard and help sick dolphins. They help the sick dolphins swim to the surface to breathe.

Calves need their mothers' protection.

ZOOS

The U.S. government passed the Marine Mammal Protection Act in 1972. Americans were worried that too many wild dolphins were being captured. The act protects wild dolphins. Other laws protect caught dolphins. These laws help make sure that zoos properly care for dolphins.

Dolphins are popular sights in zoos and parks. They are smart and able to learn tricks quickly. Once, wild dolphins were caught and brought to zoos. Now, many zoos and parks have special breeding programs. Dolphins give birth to young in the zoos. Today, most zoos do not catch wild dolphins.

Scientists are studying captured dolphins. They are trying to understand how dolphins use whistles. Some scientists believe that each dolphin has its own whistle. Only that dolphin uses and makes the whistle.

Dolphins are popular sights at zoos and parks.

Helping People

Some people feel that dolphins and humans share a special bond. There are many stories of dolphins helping people. Scientists are not sure if the stories are true. They do not have an explanation for the dolphins' behaviors.

One of the stories is about the Imragen people. They live near the Sahara desert. Sometimes the Imragen see groups of fish along the shore. Then they beat the surface of the water with sticks. The noise attracts dolphins from the sea.

The dolphins push the fish toward the land. The Imragen throw their fishing nets into the water. They catch hundreds of fish at one time. Dolphins eat the fish the Imragen do not eat. It is a team effort.

Another story is about several American soldiers during World War II. The men were lost at sea in a lifeboat. Dolphins saved them by pushing the soldiers' lifeboat to shore.

Some people feel dolphins and humans share a bond.

Killer Whales

Many people do not know that killer whales are really dolphins. These whales are the largest members of the dolphin family. Killer whales can grow as long as 30 feet (nine meters).

They are called killer because they are excellent hunters. They can even kill blue whales. Blue whales are the largest animals on earth.

In the past, people called these dolphins whale killers. In time, the name was switched to killer whale. People were afraid of them because of their ability to kill. Today, scientists know that killer whales can be friendly. These large dolphins are popular sights at ocean parks like Sea World.

Killer whales are the largest dolphins in the world.

Hands On: Echolocation

Dolphins locate things in the water by using echolocation. You can use sound to locate a friend.

What You Need

One friend
One handkerchief to use as a blindfold
A large space

What You Do

1. Blindfold yourself.
2. Have your friend stand about 10 feet (three meters) away from you.
3. Your friend should begin clicking his or her fingers. Have your friend move around you.
4. Can you tell where your friend is standing? Can you tell how far away your friend is?
5. Now let your friend have a turn being blindfolded. Click your fingers in different places around your friend. Who was better at locating the other person?

You can try this with more friends. Have your friends move farther away. Is it easier or harder to decide where your friends are?

Words to Know

cetacean (si-TAY-shuhn)—the scientific name for all whales, dolphins, and porpoises
dorsal fin (DOR-suhl FIN)—the fin that sticks up from the middle of a dolphin's back
echolocation (ek-oh-loh-KAY-shuhn)—using sounds to locate objects and food
flipper (FLIP-ur)—the armlike body parts on the sides of a dolphin; used to keep balance while swimming
fluke (FLOOK)—a dolphin's tail
pod (POD)—a group of dolphins

Read More

Behrens, June. *Dolphins*. Chicago: Children's Press, 1989.

Brust, Beth Wagner. *Dolphins and Porpoises*. Mankato, Minn.: Creative Education, 1990.

American Cetacean Society
P.O. Box 2639
San Pedro, CA 90731

Wild Dolphin Project
P.O. Box 3839
Palos Verdes, CA 90274

Internet Sites

Cetacean Page Just for Children
http://www.premier1.net/~iamdavid/children.html

Mandurah Dolphins Index
http://www.southwest.com.au/~kirbyhs/madolpf2.html

Index